The New Crew's Pocketbook

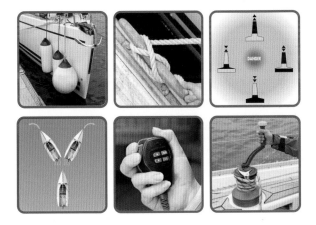

A pocket guide for newcomers to cruising: from your first sail to becoming a key crew member

Tim Davison

FERNHURST|BOOKS

www.fernhurstbooks.com

Published in 2021 by Fernhurst Books Limited.
The Windmill, Mill Lane, Harbury, Leamington Spa, Warwickshire.
CV33 9HP, UK
Tel: +44 (0) 1926 337488 | www.fernhurstbooks.com

A catalogue record for this book is available from the British Library
ISBN 9781912621354

Special thanks to Laser Performance, Northshore Yachts and Arcona Yachts

Illustrated by Greg Filip and Kara Thomas/PPL

All photos © Fernhurst Books Limited

Designed and typeset by Daniel Stephen
Printed in Czech Republic by Finidr

CONTENTS

Checklists, other materials and further information on spinnakers and gennakers are available online at www.fernhurstbooks.com. Search for 'New Crews Pocketbook' and click 'Additional Rescources'

Also available, a companion volume

INTRODUCTION

If you are a new crew a yacht can seem a daunting place. There are ropes everywhere, the loo has a mind of its own and the ceiling tilts to where the walls should be. Meanwhile, you are probably feeling a bit queasy and are worrying about the latest strong wind warning...

Don't worry! Everyone feels like this at first. *The New Crew's Pocketbook* will give you the basic knowledge to work the boat, be safe, have fun... and be asked back for more. I have used the correct terms througout, e.g. halyard, but most are defined in the Jargon Buster on pages 76-80 or on the diagrams on pages 16-18.

With this book in your pocket I hope you will have as many happy hours afloat as I have.

If you have done a bit of crewing this book will serve as a useful aide memoire to the basics, and should teach you a few new skills. If you have mastered everything here you will be a welcome addition to any crew, and will be feted by skippers to help sail their beautiful yachts to wonderful destinations!

If you are a skipper you will realise that as soon as people step on board, they are effectively crewing. They will immediately be drawn into casting off, tying knots, hoisting sails, winching and even steering. It's impossible to go over everything in your briefing, and any knowledge they can gain beforehand is a blessing. This book was devised to be given to new crew to read before they arrive at the dock. If you are lucky they might even practise their knots by the fire and try coiling and throwing a rope in their garden! On passage they can refer to it again, consolidating the teaching you will inevitably be doing under way.

Tim Davison

NB. Crews and skippers can be male or female, I just use 'he' for brevity – 'she' is also implied throughout. Boats are always 'she'.

WHAT TO BRING

So you've been invited to go sailing. Excellent! Like the rest of us you will inevitably get hooked and spend the rest of your life planning trips, buying gear and dreaming of sleek yachts.

Opposite is a list of things to take. Remember, space is limited on a yacht. Just take enough stuff so you have a change if you get wet, will be warm if the weather nosedives and cool if the sun shines. You can always wash your clothes in a marina. Pack your kit in a soft bag (NOT a suitcase) so the bag itself can be folded and stowed. Keep everything in your cabin, don't strew things about the boat or you will lose them, particularly when she heels.

Make sure you understand the arrangement: is bedding provided, are there spare waterproofs on the boat, is there a lifejacket for you? Are you expected to bring some food, and will there be a kitty to cover food, diesel and mooring fees? When and where will the trip finish, and what is the Plan B for horrid weather?

Ready for anything: cap inside hood, lifejacket, waterproofs, gloves and wellies.

That's better! Cap, sunglasses, sunblock, shorts and deck shoes.

CHECKLIST: FIRST TRIP

- ☐ Sleeping bag
- ☐ Sleeping bag liner
- ☐ Pillowcase
- ☐ Towel
- ☐ Washing & shaving kit
- ☐ Sunblock
- ☐ Seasickness pills, e.g. Stugeron
- ☐ Wet wipes
- ☐ Polythene bags
- ☐ Torch
- ☐ Batteries
- ☐ Pen & notebook
- ☐ Knife
- ☐ A float for your keys (when you drop them overboard!)

- ☐ Mobile phone & 12V charger
- ☐ Book & games (if stormbound)
- ☐ Present for the boat, e.g. cake, booze

- ☐ Shoes (2 pairs, one for afloat & one for ashore)
- ☐ Wellies (non-slip soles)
- ☐ Socks (aircraft socks dry quickly)
- ☐ Trousers
- ☐ Shorts
- ☐ Underwear
- ☐ Shirts
- ☐ Sweaters
- ☐ Neckwarmer
- ☐ Sailing gloves
- ☐ Woolly hat
- ☐ Sunhat
- ☐ Cap
- ☐ Sunglasses
- ☐ Waterproof clothing
- ☐ Mid-layers
- ☐ Swimming costume
- ☐ Consider goggles & snorkel (or are these provided?)

- ☐ Passport
- ☐ Insurance certificate
- ☐ UK Global Health Insurance Card (GHIC)
- ☐ Driving licence
- ☐ Money & credit cards
- ☐ Rail or air tickets

To download: visit www.fernhurstbooks.com. Search for '*New Crew's Pocketbook*' & click on 'Additional Resources'

HOMEWORK

The idea of this section is to give you a bit of homework so you arrive at the dock with some useful background knowledge.

Wouldn't it be more impressive if you knew how to tie some basic knots, could coil and throw a rope, and were able to name the parts of the boat? Here are some things you can work on at home, to get ahead of the game.

Round turn & two half hitches
Use: Attaching a rope to a ring or post.

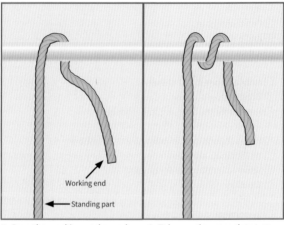

1. Pass the working end round the object.

2. Take another complete turn.

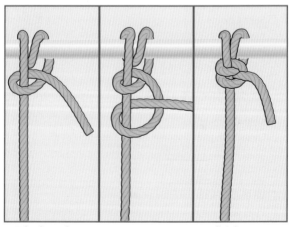

3. Take the end over the standing part, around it and back through to form a half hitch.

4. Repeat, to form a second half hitch.

5. Pull tight.

Clove hitch

Use: Attaching a rope to a ring or post.

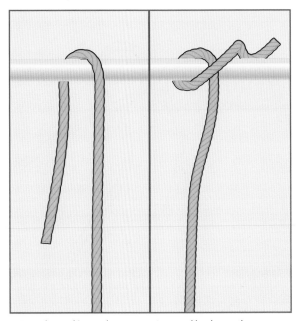

1. Pass the working end over the object...

2. ... and back over the standing part.

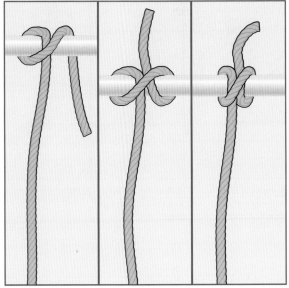

3. Pass the working end around the object again...

4. ... and back through the loop.

5. Pull tight.

Figure of eight

Use: As a stopper knot. Stops the end of a rope being pulled through a cleat or fairlead.

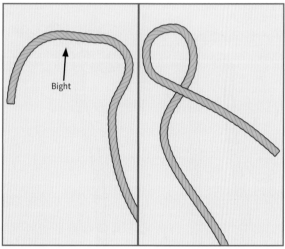

1. Make a bight.

2. Pass the working end over the standing part to form a loop.

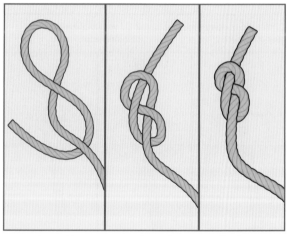

3. Pass the working end under the standing part.

4. Pass the working end through the top loop.

5. Pull tight.

Bowline

Use: Making a secure loop in a rope.

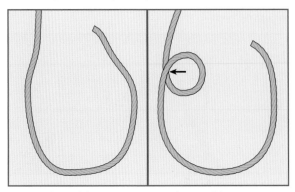

1. Form a bight of the required size.

2. Make a small loop.

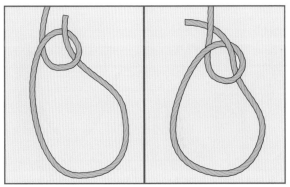

3. Pass the end up through the small loop…

4. … under the standing part…

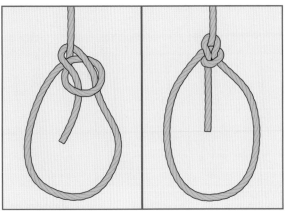

5. … and down through the small loop.

6. Pull tight and check there is a long tail.

Coiling a rope

The secret is to twist and coil the rope in a clockwise direction to stop it kinking. Finish with two or more turns and push the end through the loop.

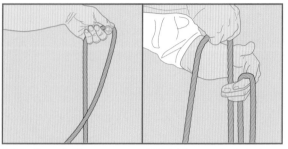

1. Take the end of the rope in your left hand.

2. Twist the rope clockwise in your right hand and transfer the rope to your left hand.

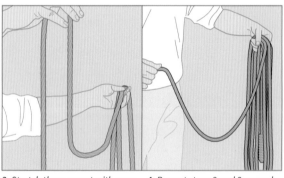

3. Stretch the rope out with your right hand.

4. Repeat steps 2 and 3 several times.

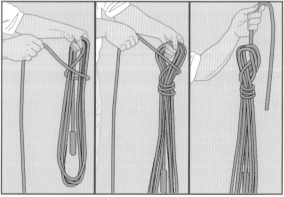

5. After you've coiled the rope take the working end around the coils.

6. Make several turns.

7. Put the working end through the loop and pull.

Throwing a rope

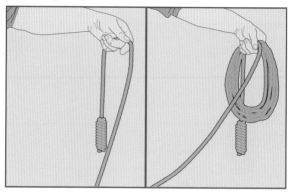

1. Take one end (weighted if necessary) in your left hand.

2. Make about eight small coils.

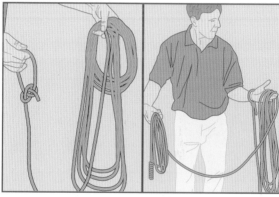

3. Then make larger coils with the rest of the rope. Make a small bowline in the end.

4. Separate the larger coils and put them in your left hand with the loop over your wrist. Take the small coils in your right hand.

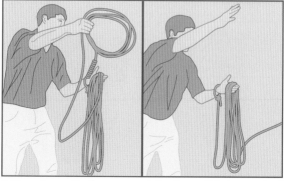

5. Throw the small coils.

6. Let them pull the large coils off your open left hand.

Cleating a rope

Use: Securing a rope temporarily so it can be undone easily.

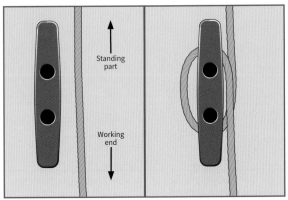

1. Bring the rope to the cleat.   *2. Make a dry turn (once around).*

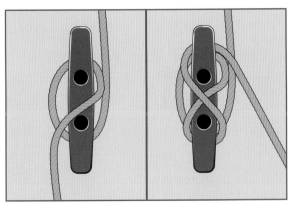

3. Begin to make a figure of eight…   *4. … and complete it.*

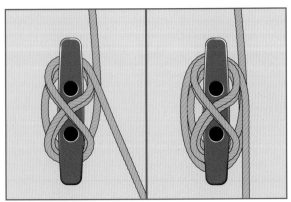

5. Make another figure of eight.   *6. Make another dry turn.*

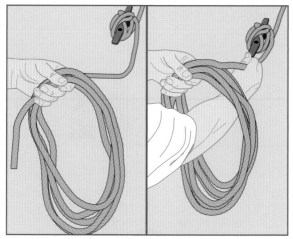

7. To finish off, coil the rope.

8. Put your hand through the coil.

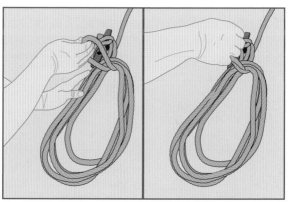

9. Pull back a loop.

10. Twist it twice.

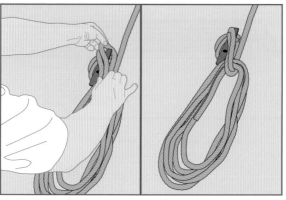

11. Hang the twisted loop over the cleat.

12. There you go – secure, neat and tidy.

PARTS OF A YACHT

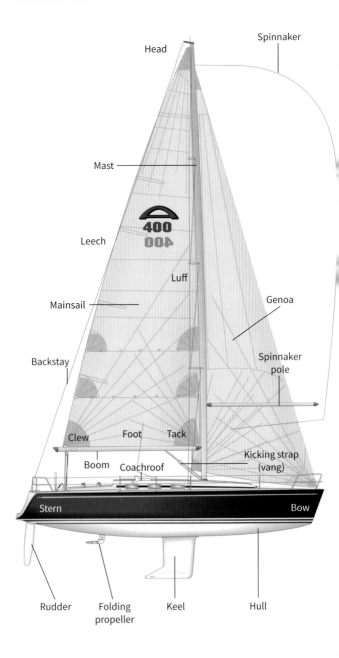

Spinnaker

Head

Mast

Leech

Luff

Genoa

Mainsail

Spinnaker pole

Backstay

Clew   Foot   Tack

Kicking strap (vang)

Boom   Coachroof

Stern   Bow

Rudder   Folding propeller   Keel   Hull

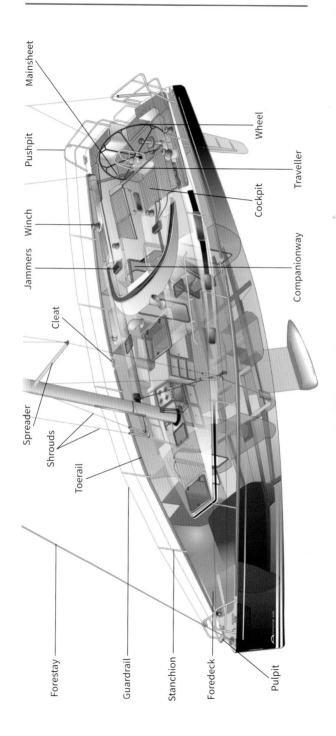

Mainsheet

Wheel

Pushpit

Traveller

Cockpit

Winch

Companionway

Jammers

Cleat

Spreader

Shrouds

Toerail

Forestay

Guardrail

Stanchion

Foredeck

Pulpit

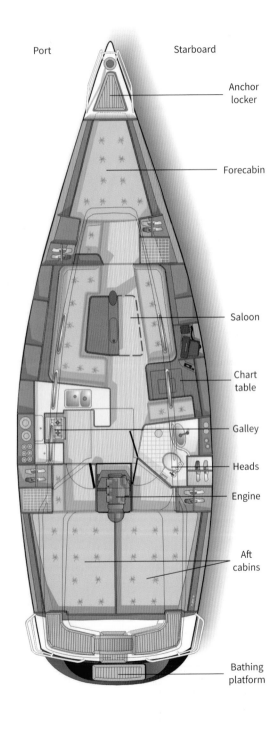

Port

Starboard

Anchor locker

Forecabin

Saloon

Chart table

Galley

Heads

Engine

Aft cabins

Bathing platform

GETTING ON & OFF

If the boat is alongside a pontoon, it is relatively easy to get on and off.

Getting on with the boat alongside

Ask whether you should take off your shoes. Then pass your bag to someone already on board and walk to the shroud. Don't grab the guardrail.

1. Lean forward and grab the shroud, put one foot on the toerail and pull yourself up.

2. Transfer your second foot to the toerail.

3. Put one leg over the guardrail, onto the deck.

4. Repeat with the other leg.

If the boats are rafted alongside each other and you have to cross one or more yachts to get to your own, the etiquette is to ask permission to come aboard, then walk across their foredeck (not through their cockpit).

Getting off with the boat alongside

You will probably be asked to get off while taking a line ashore.

1. Coil the rope and make sure that it is led correctly. When you are ashore, the line should run straight from the cleat on the boat to the cleat on the dock, NOT over the guardrail.

2. Walk to the shroud and hold it with one hand. The rope is in your other hand.

3. As you approach the dock, transfer one leg over the guardrail, then the other. You are now standing on the outside of the guardrail, still holding the shroud.

4. If the boat has high sides, squat down so you don't have so far to step.

5. As the boat slides alongside, STEP onto the dock. Don't jump! If the boat is too far away, the skipper will come round again.

6. As soon as you land, take a turn around a cleat or bollard so you can control the boat. Never stand there holding the rope straight from the yacht – it's heavier than you! Surge the rope until the boat comes to a standstill. Then pull the boat alongside.

7. Finally, secure the rope to a cleat.

Getting on & off when moored stern-to

There will usually be a plank rigged up and it's just a question of teetering along it. This will be made easier if someone pulls on the mooring rope to bring the boat closer. If you feel unsure, ask for the bow line or anchor line to be eased and the boat pulled in. Better that than a damp arrival!

Getting on from the dinghy

Often you will board at the stern of the yacht. Another crewperson will pull the dinghy tightly to the yacht and you can then step aboard. Climb up at the shrouds if boarding from alongside.

Getting into the dinghy

Again, make sure someone is holding the dinghy tightly to the yacht. Step into the middle of the dinghy or you may capsize it. Sit down immediately to aid stability.

THE SKIPPER'S BRIEFING

Before you set off the skipper will brief the crew.

Where everything is
The skipper will go through the boat, pointing out where everything is kept. You may like to use the space below to make notes of where important items are stored.

WHERE TO FIND THINGS	
Item	Location

To download: visit www.fernhurstbooks.com. Search for '*New Crew's Pocketbook*' & click on 'Additional Resources'

Safety equipment
The skipper will also point out all the safety equipment such as fire extinguishers, jackstays, lifejackets / harnesses, tethers, lifelines, liferaft, dan buoy, throwing line, retrieval line, rescue sling, flares and tools.

Flares

Flares have a variety of mechanisms and uses. Your skipper
will explain how and when they should be used. Wear gloves if
possible. Two common mechanisms are 'twist and strike' and 'pin
and push'. Always read the instructions.

Twist & Strike

1. Twist the end.

2. Strike the base firmly.

Pin & Push

*1. The arrows indicate which
way is up.*

*2. Take off the caps from
both ends.*

3. Remove the pin.

*4. Push lever
firmly upwards.*

Personal safety kit

The skipper will issue you with a lifejacket / harness and help you adjust it. Ask someone to open it up and make sure the gas cylinder is screwed in properly. He will tell you where and when to clip on your lifeline and demonstrate how to move about the boat safely.

Now is the time to try on any waterproof clothing you are borrowing and find out where it should be hung when wet.

Operating the toilet

It's vital to know how the toilet (heads) works! If you are lucky, it will simply be a question of pulling a lever one way and pumping water through, then pushing it the other way and pumping the bowl dry. But sometimes the skipper likes the seacocks shut after use (which closes off the pipes leading through the hull). You should NEVER put tampons, sanitary towels or anything inorganic down the loo, and on some boats you are asked to put the toilet paper in a bag. The pipes are narrow, and it is all too easy to block them!

If a septic tank is fitted, waste is stored in it until you get to a pumping station or offshore (if legal).

1. The machine!

2. Switch to flush.

3. Pump water in.

4. Switch back then pump dry.

Using gas

1. Open the valve at the cylinder.

2. Open the valve near the cooker.

3. Press in the knob on the cooker.

4. Light the gas and keep the knob pressed in for 5-10 seconds until the safety cut-out has heated up.

Gas is dangerous on a boat. Always turn off the knob on the cooker after using the stove, and sometimes you will be asked to turn off the valve in the pipe and maybe at the cylinder as well.

In a marina you can probably use as much electricity, gas, fuel and water as you like, but once you have left the dock remember that these are finite.

VHF radio

This is your link to the outside world. At the briefing the skipper will show you how to turn it on, adjust the Squelch, and send a Mayday call for help. See page 70 to learn how to send a Mayday and for general VHF use.

What you can damage

- The guardrails are surprisingly weak. Push off against the toerail rather than the guardrails.
- Don't hold onto the wheel for support!
- Don't grab aerials when climbing aboard, especially over the stern.
- If you're using an electric winch, look at what it's pulling, not at the winch or button. The winch has enormous power and not much feel, so you need to see what it is doing.

What can damage you

- The boom is very hard and can swing across fast. Always duck when the boom is in motion, particularly when gybing.
- It is usually safe to hold on to wires, but not to ropes. The reason they are made of rope is that they are designed to move!
- Always put a rope round a winch before releasing it from a cleat or jammer. There could be a considerable load on it, and you will need the friction of the turns round the winch to prevent it burning through your fingers.
- You will usually need a winch to pull in a rope under strain.
- Be careful pulling up the anchor, or you may damage your back.
- Watch your toes and fingers if using a windlass to raise or lower the anchor. Wear gloves and shoes.

Seasickness

Tell the skipper if you are prone to seasickness. You can either do this at the briefing, or afterwards if you are shy. He will recommend a remedy and show you how to be sick safely (don't hang out over the side – you may follow your breakfast overboard!). Take seasickness remedies well in advance. Some people find pressure point wristbands (e.g. Seabands) effective.

Most people are best on deck, looking at the horizon. If you need to go below, get horizontal as soon as you can.

If you are feeling sick on passage, tell the skipper who will make sure you are safe. If the worst comes to the worst, remain seated and be sick into a bucket.

The plan

At the briefing the skipper will give you the overall plan for the trip, and show how he has split it into smaller 'chunks'. For each, there will be a fallback plan in case things go wrong or the weather is atrocious. He will probably enter the trip on the chartplotter using a series of waypoints so you can see the boat moving from one 'X' to another as you sail.

Weather

He will also brief you on the expected weather for the trip. The data can be obtained from the harbourmaster, the internet or the onboard Navtex, or preferably from all three. But don't forget to look out of the hatch, the Mark One Eyeball gives the best short term forecast!

THE ENGINE

Starting the engine

The engine is your secondary means of propulsion. You will be shown how to turn on the engine, put it into ahead, neutral and astern, and turn it off.

1. Push in the clutch then push the accelerator forward.

2. Start the engine.

3. Pull the lever into neutral – the clutch button will click out.

4. Push the lever forward and the boat will power ahead.

Stopping the engine

1. Put the gear lever in neutral.
2. Pull out the stop lever or press the stop button.
3. When the alarm beeps, turn the key to off.
4. Push in the stop lever if necessary.

When sailing, the gear lever is usually in reverse to stop the propeller spinning.

DOCKING & CASTING OFF

A boat is usually moored to a marina pontoon or quayside by a bow and stern line and two springs.

The bow and stern lines hold the boat in to the dock, but don't stop it moving fore and aft. The springs stop the boat moving forwards and backwards (fore and aft) but don't hold the boat in!

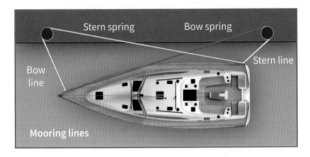

Casting off
If there is wind or tide acting on the boat, one or more of the ropes will be slack. These will be released first.

The skipper will probably now ask you to take charge of one line and double it up as a slip line. Then, as the boat heads out, you can either release one end and retrieve the line, or flip it off the cleat on the dock and pull the doubled line aboard. The key thing is not to get the rope around the propeller!

Using a slip line

1. Rig the line like this.

2. On the command, release one end and retrieve the line.

Once away, coil the rope and stow it. Then take off the fenders and stow them too.

Springing off

If the wind is strong and pushing the boat onto the dock, you may have to spring her off. You can use either a bow or a stern spring.

1. Pad the bow with lots of fenders.

2. Rig the bow spring as a slip line.

3. The boat is driven forward and the stern kicks out.

4. Retrieve the rope as the boat is reversed out.

Your job will be to hold one end of the slip line, with a turn or two on the cleat. When the boat is backing out, release this end of the line and retrieve from the other end.

Docking

You will be given one line to take ashore. Get ready as described on page 20.

As the boat arrives at the dock, step ashore and get a turn round a cleat, bollard or tree. Hold the boat, then pull her in. The easiest way to do this is to take some tension around the cleat, then pull sideways on the line, between the cleat and the boat. (You can get a lot of tension like this.) Pull the slack you have gained 'past' the cleat, and repeat. When the skipper is satisfied, cleat off the rope and go on to the next line you are given, which will probably be the spring.

1. Have the central line ready.

2. Step off.

3. Secure it to a cleat. The boat is now tethered.

4. Take the bow line.

5. Secure it.

6. Take the stern line.

7. Secure it.

8. Pull sideways on a rope to move a heavy yacht.

UNDERWAY

Steering

When you're on the helm your jobs are to keep on course, avoid hitting anything and prevent the boat running aground. If you are unsure, always call the skipper. He will prefer that to an expensive collision! Make sure you can read the depth meter and know the depth at which the boat will hit the bottom. Often an alarm is set, to warn you you're in shallow water. For example, my boat is 2.1 metres deep and grounds when the depth reads 2.1 metres, and the alarm sounds at 3.5 metres. (Some skippers prefer to have the meter show depth under the keel, so their boat grounds when the depth shows 0.)

Keep an eye on the depth readout.

Keeping on course

Marker

1. It's just like a car.
Note the marker to show the 'straight ahead' position.

2. If you want the boat to go backwards, it's easier if you steer facing aft. Now it's like steering a car once again.

If there is a suitable object ahead, you will be asked to steer for it ('head towards the smallest island'). Look straight down the centreline of the boat and steer for the object. If you want to sit off the centreline, you need to align the bow to one side of the object. (Technically, this is called parallax.) You will soon get the hang of this.

If there is no suitable object, or you are out at sea, you will be given a compass course ('steer 280'). The diagrams show how a compass works, but essentially the compass card is 'fixed' (it always points north) and you are 'steering the lubber line across it'. It's hard work looking at the compass all the time, and it may even make you feel queasy. Instead, get on course and then try to find something straight ahead – it might even be a distinctive cloud – and steer for it. The cloud will of course move, so every few minutes you need to choose a new target.

The compass card always points towards (magnetic) north. As the boat turns, the lubber line moves, and the bearing changes from 340° to 0° to 20°.

The other thing to watch is the sails. If the sails are flapping, you are either off-course or the wind has changed! Check the compass, and if you are still on course ask for the sheets to be adjusted (see page 52).

How can I steer?

You can only steer if there is a flow of water across the rudder (see diagram overleaf). When the rudder is turned, the water is deflected. The water hitting the rudder pushes it, and the back of the boat, in direction C. The bow turns to the left.

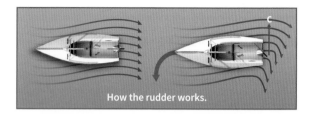

How the rudder works.

If the boat has a tiller, experiment with pushing it away from you and pulling it towards you. You push the tiller in the opposite direction to where you want to go (see diagram below).

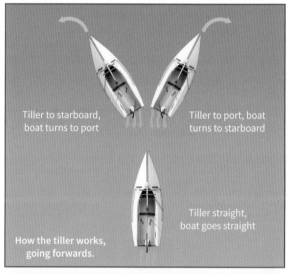

Tiller to starboard, boat turns to port

Tiller to port, boat turns to starboard

Tiller straight, boat goes straight

How the tiller works, going forwards.

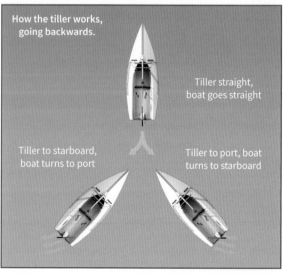

How the tiller works, going backwards.

Tiller straight, boat goes straight

Tiller to starboard, boat turns to port

Tiller to port, boat turns to starboard

Steering backwards with a tiller is tricky – begin by holding the tiller centrally so it doesn't swing hard to one side and always keep a firm grip on it. Then push the tiller towards the direction you want the bow to turn (see diagram).

Many boats have an autohelm and this can be useful on long legs. Get the skipper to show you how to switch it on and off and adjust the course. Have a practice, because if something comes up unexpectedly you will need to switch off the autohelm quickly and steer manually out of danger.

If you think a collision is possible, call the skipper early so you have time to avoid the problem.

BUOYAGE

Buoys are used in inshore waters to warn of hazards and mark the limits of navigable channels. (In busy commercial waters you may be asked to steer just outside the navigable channel.)

Lateral marks
The system of bouyage, including standard shapes, colours, etc., and used throughout Europe is known as the IALA system.

DIRECTION OF BUOYAGE – a starboard hand buoy marks the starboard side of the channel when entering harbour. This direction is usually obvious in a river but, where any doubt may exist, this symbol shows the direction of buoyage.

IALA System A (Europe, Australia, New Zealand, Africa, the Gulf & some Asian countries)

 Port hand
Light: red, any rhythm

 Starboard hand
Light: green, any rhythm

Modified lateral mark
You could go either side, but one is preferred.

 Preferred channel to starboard

 Preferred channel to port

IALA System B (North, Central & South America, Japan, North & South Korea & the Philippines)

  Port hand

  Starboard hand

Cardinal marks

Cardinal buoys indicate the direction in which a particular danger lies, and the side on which it is safe to pass.

- A north cardinal lies to the north of the danger, and the clear water is on the north of the buoy.
- The characteristics of the light follow the pattern of a clock face.

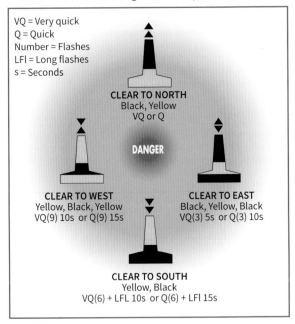

VQ = Very quick
Q = Quick
Number = Flashes
LFl = Long flashes
s = Seconds

CLEAR TO NORTH
Black, Yellow
VQ or Q

DANGER

CLEAR TO WEST
Yellow, Black, Yellow
VQ(9) 10s or Q(9) 15s

CLEAR TO EAST
Black, Yellow, Black
VQ(3) 5s or Q(3) 10s

CLEAR TO SOUTH
Yellow, Black
VQ(6) + LFL 10s or Q(6) + LFl 15s

Other marks

Isolated danger mark
Light: White Fl(2)
Isolated danger with clear
water all round.

Safe water mark
Light: Isophase or occulting or
1 long flash every 10 seconds or
Morse 'A' (• —).
Usually placed at the approach
to a channel: Shows safe water
all around.

New danger mark
Light: Alternating blue and
yellow flashing light or morse
'D' (— • •).
Identifies new dangers or
wrecks.

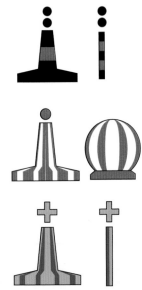

NIGHT-TIME PASSAGE

Let's assume you have been on watch in the daytime and are now turning in to your bunk but will be on watch again in a few hours, in darkness.

Before you go to sleep it's a good idea to organise your gear so you can get dressed again quickly and get on deck before you feel too queasy. Have your boots and waterproofs ready, with your lifejacket / harness adjusted to fit. If your waterproof jacket has toggles, you can have your lifejacket permanently fitted to them. Have gloves, a torch and a woolly hat handy too – it can be cold at night. In daylight, note where the strong points are for clipping on.

Set an alarm or ask the current watch to wake you ten minutes before you are due on deck. It will be a major black mark if you are late on deck. Then have a good sleep.

Sleeping

Boots and trousers ready to be stepped into.

A leecloth will hold you into your bunk.

Hopefully they will wake you with a cup of tea! Go to the loo, then get dressed fully before you stick your head out of the hatch – a rogue wave always seems to hit you just as you appear! Stand on the companion steps and clip on before you go outside – you will probably still be half asleep and you want to be safe as you emerge.

Ask the helm what has been happening, if there are any possible collisions in the offing, what the course is and how the boat is going. When you're ready, take over. The previous helm will probably watch you for a few minutes to see that you have the right idea, then they will go below for some well-earned shuteye.

You must always be clipped on at night. Never leave the cockpit unless someone is watching you. Keep a sharp lookout, in all directions. If you see the lights of another boat approaching, discuss it with your companion or call the skipper. Use the autohelm if you need to go below: you will probably need to fill in the log every hour, for example. NEVER pee over the side, because of the danger of falling off. Use the heads.

Clipping on with your tether

Clip on before you come into the cockpit.

Stay clipped on.

If you need to go forward, clip on to the jackstay.

You must be clipped on when steering too.

A quarter of an hour before the next watch, put on the kettle and make tea. Shake the next person ten minutes before their watch begins.

HOW DOES A BOAT SAIL?

Wind is the boat's driving force. The wind flows over the windward side of each sail (causing pressure) and round the leeward side (causing suction). The resulting forces on the sails act in directions A and B, at right angles to the sails.

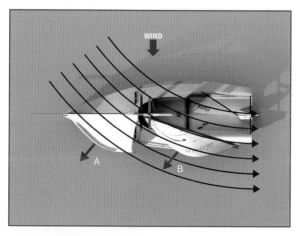

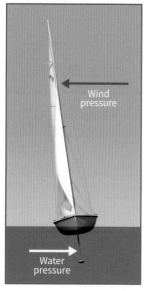

The forces push the boat forwards and sideways. The forward push is welcome! The sideways forces are counteracted by water pressure on the keel, although the boat will always drift sideways a bit.

As the boat heels, the keel begins to exert a righting effect, and the sails' forces decrease. She will automatically heel to exactly the point where the forces are in balance. Note that it is impossible for a yacht to capsize (except in extreme wave conditions) because when she is lying on her side the sails' force is zero and the keel force is maximum. So don't worry about a bit of heeling!

Of course, excessive heel is uncomfortable and makes steering difficult so the skipper will show you how to reduce heel, by letting out the sheets or reefing (reducing the sail area).

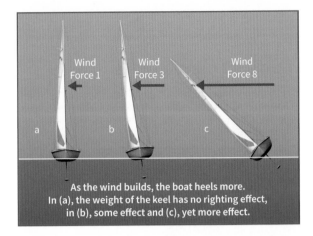

As the wind builds, the boat heels more.
In (a), the weight of the keel has no righting effect,
in (b), some effect and (c), yet more effect.

If the sails are pulled in, forces A and B are almost at right angles to the boat: the sideways force is maximum and the boat will try to heel a lot. When the sails are let out, the forces point forwards so the boat heels less. With the wind behind, there is no heeling effect (but the boat can roll!!!).

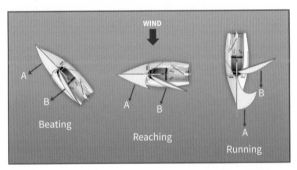

How can I stop?

It is the wind in the sails that makes the boat go forward. To stop it or slow down, take the wind out of the sails by either letting out the sheets or by altering course towards the wind, so that the sails flap.

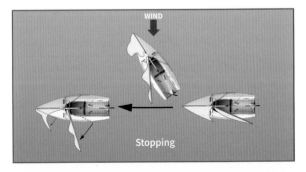

How can I tell which way the wind is blowing?

Everything in sailing is related to wind direction. You can tell which way it's blowing by the feel of it on your cheek, by the wave direction, by the wind indicator at the top of the mast or by the instruments.

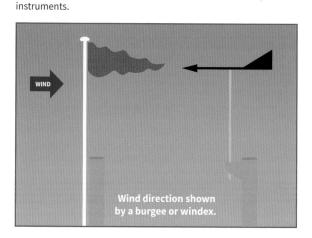

Wind direction shown by a burgee or windex.

UNDERWAY

Points of sailing – Look at the diagram below

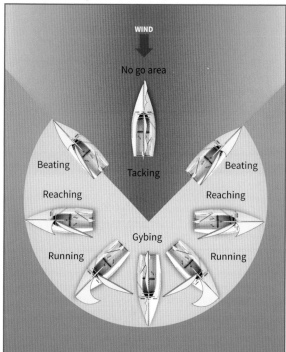

There are three points of sailing:

> **Reaching** – the boat sails across the wind
> **Beating** – the boat sails towards the wind
> **Running** – the boat sails away from the wind

Reaching
Here the boat sails at right angles to the wind, which is blowing from the windward side to the leeward side. The sails will be about halfway out.

Beating
If you want to change course towards the wind you must pull in the sails as you turn.

You can go on turning towards the wind until the sails are pulled right in. You are then beating, and in fact are sailing at about 45 degrees to the wind.

If you try to turn further towards the wind, you enter the No Go Area. The sails flap and the boat slows or stops.

If you want to get to a point upwind of your present position, you have to BEAT in a zigzag fashion.

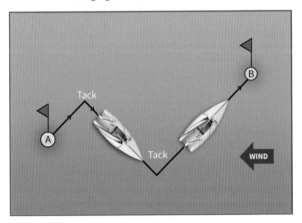

At the end of each 'zig' the boat turns through about 90°. This turn is called a TACK. The boat turns 'through' the wind – the sails blow across to the other side. The old genoa sheet is let off and the new one is winched in.

Running
From a reach you may want to change course away from the wind. Let out the sheets as you turn. You can go on turning until the wind is coming from behind the boat. You are RUNNING.

If you turn more, the boat will gybe. The wind gets behind the mainsail and whips it across with a bang, which is potentially dangerous. The best ways to gybe are covered on page 63.

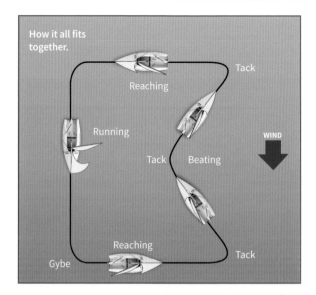

WINCHING

On a small boat like a dinghy you are quite safe to hold ropes in your hands. On a yacht you must ALWAYS use a winch to pull in or let out a rope. There could be a force of several tons on the rope and if you simply uncleat it, it will burn through your hands or pull your fingers into the cleat. Always use a winch, even in light winds, to be safe.

Since you will be using the winches all the time, it's worth practising winching even before you set off. Get the skipper to show you how it all works.

Winches are of two types: standard and self-tailing. Nearly all modern yachts are fitted with self-tailing winches. It is possible to use a self-tailing winch as a standard winch.

Ropes must go clockwise round a winch. A quick spin with your hands will remind you which way the rope should be led.

Use a winch handle to wind a winch that is under load. Most winches are geared. Wind clockwise initially and when the handle becomes hard to turn, wind anticlockwise. Winch handles normally lock in place when inserted into a winch. Ask the skipper to show you how to remove the handle, as the mechanisms vary.

Self-tailing winches
Self-tailing winches have a gripper arrangement on top. Take three or four clockwise turns of the rope around the winch, starting at the bottom and working upwards with each turn. Put the rope over the metal arm, then pull into the gripper and loop around. You can now let go of the rope and use two hands for winding!

If the rope slips, take another turn around the winch. Always watch what is happening at the other end of the rope. A sail may be snagged, and if you keep on winding you could tear it. Always look at what you are pulling in, not at the winch.

1. Put on the turns then lead the rope over the arm and into the gripper

2. Put in the handle and wind.

Standard winches

Here we are using a self-tailing winch as a standard winch. Take three or four turns around the winch. Since you are not using the gripper to hold the rope, you must keep tension on it using your hand. Another crew member can pull the end of the rope for you, this is called 'tailing'. When the sail has been hoisted, sheet pulled in or control line tightened, the rope will need to be secured to a cleat or in a jammer to keep the tension on.

1. Take three or four turns clockwise around the drum.

2. Keep tension on, and wind.

Letting out a rope

Always use a winch to gradually loosen a rope that is under load. If the rope is secured in a jammer, first wind the rope around the winch three times and secure before lifting the jammer lever. To let a rope off a self-tailer, first free it from the gripper while keeping tension on the rope at all times. Use the palm of your left hand to push the rope anti-clockwise as you gradually ease with your right hand. Keep your fingers clear and do not allow the rope to become slack. Once most of the load has been released, the line can be allowed to run more freely, and eventually the turns can be flicked off entirely.

1. Take out the handle.

2. Take the rope out of the gripper, but keep up the tension with your right hand. Use the palm of your left hand to ease out the rope.

Electric winches

Electric winches are becoming more common. If you are a beginner, it's best not to use them, because they have no feel and it's easy to wind too far and break something at the other end of the rope. You can always insert a winch handle in an electric winch and wind in the normal way.

If you do use an electric winch, watch carefully what it is pulling, i.e. don't look at the button or the winch!

Terminology

If you are lucky, you'll simply be asked to wind in or let out a rope. But people who have done some racing talk about 'on' and 'off', e.g. 'Sheet on!' So be aware this means 'Wind in the sheet, please' (though you'll be lucky to get a please, even when cruising!).

Clearing a riding turn

Sometimes the rope gets jammed on a winch.

Tie a second rope to the first with a rolling hitch. Pull on the second rope with a winch to take the strain off the jam. Then undo the knitting.

HOISTING SAILS

We will look at how to hoist a mainsail that has been stowed along the boom and unroll a genoa from a roller-reefing furler. Some yachts will have their mainsails furled inside their mast or boom. Racing yachts will often have different headsails that are stowed in bags, then clipped or hanked onto the forestay before hoisting.

Hoisting the mainsail

1. Take off the mainsail cover, fold it up and put it away.
2. Shackle the main halyard to the top of the mainsail.
   (The halyard is the rope that pulls up the sail.)
3. The helmsman will steer the boat into the wind.
4. Make sure the mainsheet is loosened a bit and the kicking strap (vang) is loose. (The kicking strap pulls the boom down.) The topping lift should continue to be tight. (The topping lift pulls the boom up.)
5. Hoist the mainsail. One crew can pull the halyard at the mast while another winches the halyard. This is called sweating the halyard (see below). Alternatively, you can simply winch up the halyard. Watch the sail carefully, rather than looking at the winch. Stop when the halyard reaches its mark, or the luff (front edge) of the sail goes tight.
6. Tighten the kicking strap (vang) and loosen the topping lift slightly.
7. The helmsman can now point the yacht out of the No Go Zone and pull in the mainsheet until the sail stops flapping.

Working as a team to sweat up the mainsail

1. The mast person pulls the halyard sideways.

2. Then the cockpit person pulls in the slack.

3. When the mainsail is up, and the halyard is at its mark, the halyard is secured in the jammer.

Unwinding the jib or genoa

1. *One person keeps some tension on the furling line, while the other pulls the jibsheet on the winch.*

2. *Put the jibsheet into the gripper then wind*

TRIMMING THE SAILS

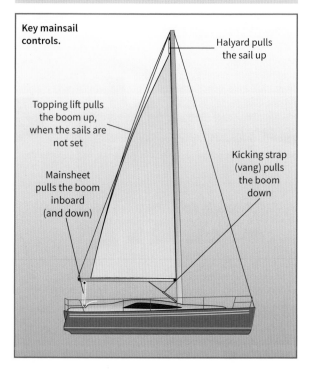

Key mainsail controls.

Halyard pulls the sail up

Topping lift pulls the boom up, when the sails are not set

Kicking strap (vang) pulls the boom down

Mainsheet pulls the boom inboard (and down)

Let's look at how to trim the sails in moderate winds on a beat, reach and run. Any differences in light and heavy winds are dealt with at the end of each section.

Trimming on a beat
Wind in the leeward genoa sheet using the leeward winch.

To do this take three turns clockwise round the winch. Hold the sheet or, if you are using a self-tailing winch, take the sheet over the metal arm and pull it into the gripper on top of the winch. Then insert the winch handle and wind. As you wind, look up the leech (back edge) of the genoa and continue until the leech is a few inches off the spreader.

Now centralise the mainsheet traveller and pull in the mainsheet. Look at the telltales on the leech of the sail and continue to pull until the top ones stop flying horizontally behind the sail. In light winds you won't need to pull too hard, but in strong winds it may take all your strength.

Now ask the helmsman if the helm is balanced. If he has weather helm (the boat is trying to turn into the wind) drop the traveller to leeward. If he has lee helm, or wants more power, pull the traveller up to windward. The boom should never go to windward of the boat's centreline.

Trim the genoa by looking at the leech (back edge) while winching. There should be a two inch gap between the leech and the spreader.

To trim the mainsheet, watch the mark on the wheel. If the helmsman is having to bear away constantly (turn away from the wind), drop the traveller to leeward until the wheel straightens up.

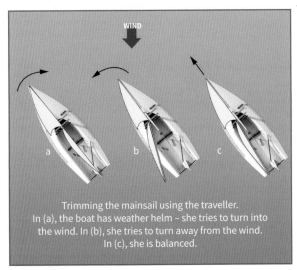

Trimming the mainsail using the traveller.
In (a), the boat has weather helm – she tries to turn into the wind. In (b), she tries to turn away from the wind.
In (c), she is balanced.

Telltales

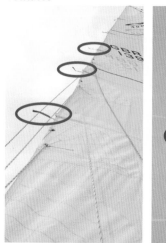

On a beat, the top telltales on the main should stream about half the time. The telltales on the genoa should stream on both sides.

Trimming on a reach

Ease out the genoa sheet until the front of the sail starts to flap. Alternatively, ease until the windward telltale starts to stop streaming (see diagram). As you ease, look at the sail, not the winch.

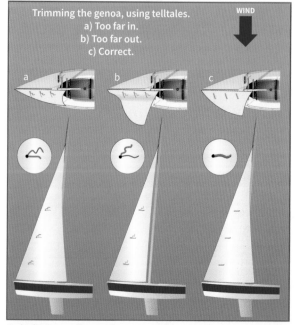

Trimming the genoa, using telltales.
a) Too far in.
b) Too far out.
c) Correct.

WIND

Red telltale port (leeward)
Green telltale starboard (windward)

To ease the sheet take it out of the cleat or the gripper on top of the winch. Put one hand round the coils, as shown on page 48, and slowly ease out with the other hand. This technique prevents the sheet getting jammed – i.e. prevents a riding turn.

Now put the handle into the winch and wind until the front of the sail just stops flapping. Alternatively, wind until the telltales are streaming on both sides of the genoa. You now have the genoa trimmed nicely, with airflow over both sides of the sail.

Finally, let out the mainsheet until the front of the sail begins to flap, then pull in again until it just stops flapping. The boom will be roughly in line with the Windex / burgee.

Trimming on a run

Let out the mainsheet until the boom is against the shroud. (Some skippers like you to pull it in a bit further, to prevent the sail chafing against the shroud and spreaders.) Note that there is no flow around the sail on a run, so the telltales are useless.

In light winds someone can stand with his back to the boom to hold it out, though if the boat is going that slowly the skipper will probably drop the sails and motor.

In strong winds it's wise to rig a preventer (see diagram). This holds out the boom as the boat rolls. The preventer is led aft so it can be released after an accidental gybe. You must, of course, take it off before a controlled gybe, and re-rig it on the other side after the gybe.

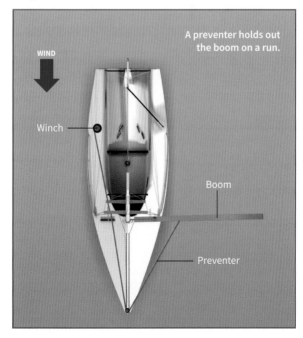

WIND

A preventer holds out the boom on a run.

Winch

Boom

Preventer

Setting the genoa is a problem, because it is in the wind shadow of the mainsail and gets no wind. Often there is a wind swirl behind the main, and the genoa misbehaves. You have five options:

1. Try to set the genoa so it is as far out as possible without flapping. The more the helmsman steers towards the wind, the more the sail will fill.
2. Roll up half the genoa, and then set it as above. At least this stops the genoa flapping against the mast fittings.
3. Roll up the genoa completely and sail under mainsail alone.
4. Pole out the genoa on the windward side. The easiest way to do this is to roll up the genoa. Rig the spinnaker pole as shown in the photos, with the windward genoa sheet through the jaws on the end of the pole. When all is ready, pull the windward sheet to unwind the genoa. You are now sailing goosewinged.
5. Set the spinnaker. (See page 68.)

Goosewinging the jib or genoa

1. Roll up the genoa.

2. Put the new (windward) sheet through the pole's jaws.

3. Clip the pole to the mast.

4. Hold the pole until the sail is unrolled.

5. The sail now sets nicely on the opposite side to the mainsail.

REEFING

Reefing is making the sails smaller. This makes the boat heel less and balances the helm. You gradually reduce sail as the wind builds.

1. The simplest way to begin is by rolling up a bit of genoa. Let out the genoa sheet just enough so the furling line can be pulled (or winched) in.
2. Then put in the first reef in the mainsail (see opposite). Ask the helmsman to sail on a close reach. Then:
   a. Tighten the topping lift.
   b. Let out the kicking strap (vang).
   c. Slacken the mainsheet slightly.
   d. Let off the main halyard enough for the sail to drop to the first reefing point. The halyard should have been marked to show how far to lower it.
   e. Pull down the first, forward reefing line or go forward and put the cringle (metal eye) onto the reefing hook.
   f. Wind down the first, aft reefing line.
   g. Tighten the halyard, let off the topping lift a little and tighten the kicking strap (vang).
   h. Finally, trim the mainsheet.
3. Put in the second reef.
4. Put in the third reef.

Some boats have in-mast or in-boom reefing for the mainsail. With in-mast reefing you essentially roll the mainsail onto a spindle inside the mast like a giant roller blind. The mainsail has been specially cut for this, and has vertical battens or no battens at all.

1. The skipper will arrange the topping lift so the boom is at the right angle.
2. Let off the mainsheet a bit.
3. Let off the kicking strap (vang).
4. Pull the furling line. This rolls up some of the mainsail and lets off the outhaul at the same time.

To let out a reef in the genoa, gradually let out the furling line while winching in the sheet.

To let out a reef in the mainsail first ask the helmsman to sail on a close reach. Then:
1. Let out the mainsheet a little.
2. Take the aft reefing line around a winch and let it out.
3. Let off the kicking strap (vang).
4. Release the halyard a bit.
5. Release the forward reefing line or go forward and take the cringle off the hook.
6. Pull up the halyard, to the mark.
7. Tighten the kicking strap (vang).
8. Trim the mainsheet.

Reefing the mainsail

1. Let off the vang (kicking strap) and the mainsheet a little, and lower the halyard to its mark.

2. Winch in the reefing lines.

3. Finally, tighten the halyard and vang, and adjust the mainsheet.

If your boat has a topping lift, tension it before you begin – to prevent the boom from hitting you on the head.

TACKING

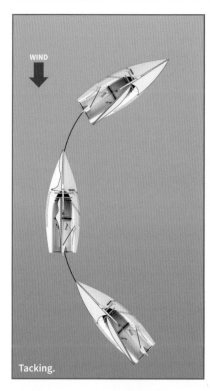

WIND

Tacking.

During a tack the boat turns slowly 90 degrees 'through' the wind. The mainsail blows across to the new leeward side. The genoa also blows across but you need to release the old genoa sheet and pull in the new one as the boat turns.

The simplest way to handle the mainsail is to leave the sheet cleated throughout. Arrange the traveller lines so the car slides to the correct spot on the new tack, or adjust it after the tack.

Tacking the genoa with one crew

1. The helmsman warns 'Ready about?'
2. Make sure there is a winch handle handy by the 'new' winch.
3. Make sure the old sheet you will be releasing is not tangled, and the new sheet has a couple of turns on the new winch.
4. Grab the sheet and take a turn off the winch while keeping the tail under tension. Hold this sheet.
5. Reply 'Ready'.
6. The helmsman says 'Lee oh' or 'Lets go' or, if you're unlucky, just turns!
7. Wait until the boat has reached the head-to-wind position.
8. Smartly flick the old sheet off the winch and make sure it has no kinks so it can run out.
9. Pull hard on the new sheet.
10. When you can pull no more, take another turn round the winch. Keep the rope under tension and your fingers clear of the winch.
11. Put in the winch handle and wind.
12. Watch the leech of the genoa. Stop winding when it is a couple of inches off the spreader.
13. Cleat the sheet. Take a bow. You have just made yourself indispensable!

1. *Take a sheet in each hand. Let off the old sheet.*

2. Pull in the new sheet as the boat turns.

3. *Take an extra turn on the winch.*

4. *Wind the sheet home.*

Tacking the genoa with two people

If you are lucky enough to have two people to tack the genoa, one (A) can control the new sheet leaving the other (B) to let off the old sheet, then cross the cockpit and wind the new winch. So have the strongest person on the old sheet to begin with.

The most efficient way to tack is with two people. The person in red pulls in the new sheet, then puts on a further turn, whilst the person in blue lets off the old sheet, brings the handle across the boat and winches in the new sheet.

1. The helmsman warns 'Ready about?'
2. B makes sure there is a winch handle by his side.
3. The crew make sure the old sheet is not tangled, and the new sheet has a couple of turns on the new winch.
4. B takes a turn off the winch and holds this sheet. A holds the new sheet.
5. You both reply 'Ready'.
6. The helmsman says 'Lee oh'.
7. Wait until the boat has reached the head-to-wind position.
8. B smartly flicks the old sheet off the winch and makes sure it has no kinks so it can run out.
9. A pulls hard on the new sheet.
10. When A can pull no more, he takes another turn round the winch and continues pulling.
11. B crosses the boat, puts in the winch handle and winds. With A pulling and B winding the genoa soon comes in.
12. B watches the leech of the genoa and stops winding when it is a couple of inches off the spreader.
13. A can now cleat the sheet.

GYBING

The problem with gybing is that, with the wind behind, the mainsail is constantly powered up and can swing across viciously. The crew's job is to control it. Note that a gybe is quite unlike a tack, where the sails flap harmlessly as the bow turns 'through' the wind.

1. Cleat the traveller centrally.

2. Pull in the mainsheet (on this boat you winch it in).

3. After the gybe, pay out the mainsheet.

4. Let off the old jibsheet and trim the new one.

To make a successful gybe:

1. The helmsman calls 'Ready to gybe?'
2. Take off the boom preventer (if rigged).
3. Pull the mainsheet traveller into the middle of the track, and firmly cleat both control lines. (This is important, or the traveller will shoot across the track in the gybe, catching someone's fingers.)
4. Make sure no-one is near the traveller or the area the mainsheet will traverse.
5. Call 'Ready'.
6. Now pull in all the mainsheet, until the boom is lying down the centreline of the boat, and cleat the mainsheet.
7. The helmsman now calls 'Gybe oh' and bears away until the boom blows across to the new side. Everyone ducks!
8. Meanwhile the new genoa sheet is pulled in, then the old one released.
9. Finally, the mainsheet is slowly paid out so the boom swings out on the new side.
10. Re-rig the boom preventer, if needed.

If it's windy you will need to wear sailing gloves to handle the mainsheet.

The helmsman is an important team member. He needs to steer a steady course just off downwind while the gybe is being set up, then turn slowly and steadily until the wind blows the boom across. Finally, he immediately needs to get back to the proper new course, just off downwind. (The boat may try to skew round onto a reach at this point, which the helmsman must firmly resist.)

Some boats have runners, and this makes things more complicated. Runners are ropes or wires that help support the mast. They have one end attached to the mast near the top of the genoa and the other is secured near the back of the boat. The lower ends have a block and tackle, so each runner can be tightened or loosened.

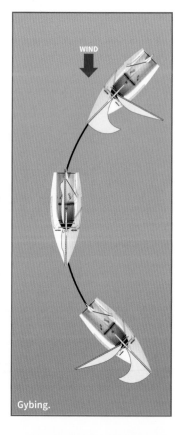

WIND

Gybing.

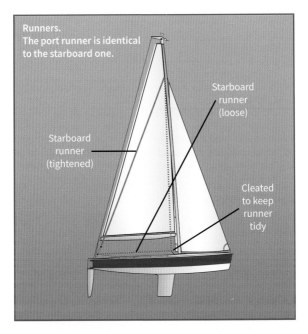

Runners.
The port runner is identical to the starboard one.

Starboard runner (loose)

Starboard runner (tightened)

Cleated to keep runner tidy

When the boat is running with the boom on the port side, the port runner will be slack and the starboard runner tight. As the boom is pulled in to gybe, the port runner is also pulled tight. Before the boom goes across, the starboard runner must be let right off or the boom can't go out on the new side. As a beginner, you may well be given the runners to operate. Talk the procedure through with the skipper before the gybe begins, but the crucial thing is to let off the old runner before the boom comes across!

LOWERING SAILS

At the end of a trip you will normally lower the sails and motor to the marina or anchorage.

1. Firstly, roll up the genoa.
2. Check that there are no ropes over the side, then start the engine and motor slowly ahead.
3. Ease out the kicking strap (vang) and pull up the topping lift a bit. This will prevent the boom dropping when the mainsail comes down.
4. Pull in the mainsheet as the boat turns head-to-wind. Pull it tight and cleat it, or the boom will fly around while you are trying to flake the mainsail along the boom.
5. Check that the main hatch is shut, or you will fall through! Take some sail ties with you onto the coachroof (cabin roof).
6. Go to the mast. Ask for the main halyard to be let off so you can pull down the front edge of the mainsail. (If you're on a big boat, you may need to climb steps on the mast to reach the sail.)
7. Now walk aft along the coachroof, then start to concertina the

aft end of the mainsail onto the boom.

8. When you have made a few tucks, tie a sail-tie around them and the boom.

9. Repeat, concertina-ing the sail and adding sail-ties as you move towards the mast.

10. Finally, take the main halyard off the mainsail and ask where it should be stowed – usually it's shackled to the aft end of the boom. (This stops the halyard flapping against the mast.)

You can usually wait to put on the sail cover(s) until the boat is tied up. Now all you have to do is put out some fenders on each side of the boat, rig the bow and stern lines and enjoy the view as you come into the harbour!

Furling the genoa

1. Uncleat the furling line and genoa sheet.

2. Pull in the furling line, making sure the sheet runs out freely. Finally coil up the furling line.

Dropping the main

1. Let off the halyard.

2. Pull down the sail.

3. Shut the hatch.

4. Take the sail ties with you.

5. Concertina the sail and hold it in place with the sail ties.

6. Work forward from the end of the boom to the mast.

SPINNAKERS & GENNAKERS

Spinnakers can be difficult to handle, but give a memorable ride.
Gennakers are much easier to handle.

Spinnakers

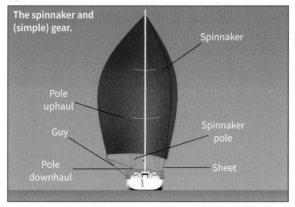

The spinnaker and (simple) gear.
Spinnaker
Pole uphaul
Guy
Spinnaker pole
Pole downhaul
Sheet

The pole is always on the opposite side to the boom. It is held up
by an uphaul, and down by a downhaul. Both need to be tight, to
stop the pole bouncing up and down.

The guy goes from a winch in the cockpit, through the end of
the pole and to the windward corner of the spinnaker. The pole
spreads out the spinnaker. When you winch the guy aft it pulls the
spinnaker and the pole around to the windward side.

The sheet goes from the cockpit to the leeward corner of the
spinnaker. It works like the sheet on any sail – you let it out until
the sail curls, then pull it in until the sail just fills.

The halyard goes from the top of the spinnaker to a pulley up the
mast, then down and back to a winch. It pulls up the spinnaker.

Lazy sheets & guys
You may have a sheet and a guy on each side – i.e. four ropes in all.
Only one rope on each side of the boat is used at a time.

In the diagram the guy is tight on the port (windward) side and the
sheet on the starboard (leeward) side. The opposite one is lose –
called 'lazy'.

The two guys and two sheets mean:
a. The lead for each guy is forward, which helps pull down on the
   windward corner of the spinnaker.
b. The lead for each sheet is aft which allows the leeward side of
   the spinnaker to fly.
c. When gybing the spinnaker, you take the tension on both
   sheets. This gives slack guys, which is very useful when trying to
   get the pole end off one and onto the other.

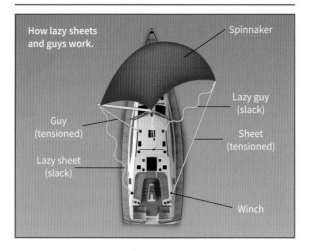

How lazy sheets and guys work.

Spinnaker

Guy (tensioned)

Lazy guy (slack)

Sheet (tensioned)

Lazy sheet (slack)

Winch

Gennakers

A gennaker is a cross between a spinnaker and a genoa.

The tack of the gennaker is attached right at the front of the boat.

The two sheets are rigged like the sheets of a genoa, but led so the sail can be gybed across in front of the forestay.

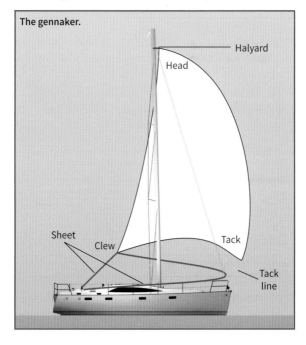

The gennaker.

Halyard

Head

Sheet

Clew

Tack

Tack line

Details about handling spinnakers and gennakers are available online at www.fernhurstbooks.com. Search for *New Crew's Pocketbook* and click on 'Additional Resources'.

MAYDAY

Sending a Mayday call

If your situation is such that there is grave and imminent danger to the ship or a person, send a Mayday call on channel 16.

1. You will need to know where you are. Use one of the following:
a. Look at the chart and see roughly where the boat is e.g. '170 degrees true FROM Beachy Head, 7 miles'.
b. Look at the GPS or chartplotter and read the latitude and longitude e.g. '50 degrees 22 decimal 47 minutes north, 001 degrees 26 decimal 80 east' (50° 22'. 47N 001° 26'. 80E).
2. Switch on the radio at the control panel and at the set.
3. Select channel 16.
4. Press the 1w/25w button until 25w is displayed.
5. Turn the Squelch until a hiss is heard, then turn it back until the hiss just disappears.
6. Pick up the handset.
7. Press and hold down the Press To Talk button and say:

> 'Mayday Mayday Mayday
>
> This is yacht...............yacht..............yacht................
>
> Callsign* and MMSI
>
> Mayday yacht ....
>
> Our position is ....
>
> We are sinking / have a man overboard / are on fire, etc.
>
> Require immediate assistance
>
> Four people on board
>
> Other vital information: e.g. we have a liferaft and are abandoning ship into it
>
> Over'

8. Release the PTT switch and wait for the reply.
9. If none comes, repeat the Mayday call.

*Your call sign is often on a label by the radio.
Or you can write it here:

_____

1. Switch on the VHF at the control panel.

2. Switch on the set.

3. Set the Squelch.

4. Press channel 16.

5. Pick up the mike. Press to talk.

6. Release the switch to listen.

Sending a Mayday on a DSC set

A set with Digital Selective Calling (DSC) has a red button under a red cover. Using this facility before sending a voice Mayday doubles your chances of being located, because the set first sends a short burst of information containing your boat's details and your position.

1. Switch on the set at the control panel and at the set itself.
2. Slide and hold back the red cover.
3. Press the red button once.
4. Then press and hold down the red button.
5. The set will count down and tell you the alert has been sent.
6. Wait 15 seconds, and the screen should show an acknowledgement.
7. In any case, after 15 seconds pick up the handset and send a voice Mayday call i.e.
   Mayday, Mayday, Mayday
   This is .... etc., etc. (see page 70).

Remember, the coastguard would rather hear about problems early than deal with emergencies later.

Mayday relay

If your radio has a greater range than the vessel in distress, you may need to rebroadcast a Mayday you have received.

"Mayday relay, Mayday relay, Mayday relay.

Dover Coastguard, Dover Coastguard, Dover Coastguard

This is Sierra, Sierra, Sierra.

Mayday received from Swift.

MMSI 233077310.

Position black rocks, Deadly Point.

Aground and breaking up.

Require immediate assistance.

White motor cruiser with 2 persons onboard.

Over."

DSC distress alert

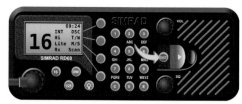

1. Open the red cover.

2. Press red button.

3. Select cause of distress, if time.

4. Press and hold the red button through the countdown.

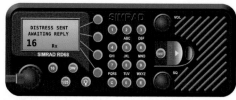

5. Wait no more than 15 seconds for the acknowledgement. Send voice Mayday on channel 16 using high power.

For speed
1. Open cover.
2. Press red button. Release.
3. Press and hold red button for 5 seconds.

MAN OVERBOARD (MOB)

Soon after you set off the skipper may give a demonstration of the MOB procedure. This varies from boat to boat and of course depends whether you are sailing or motoring (which gives an easier recovery). Here is a rough plan for a fully-crewed yacht which is sailing. I've followed it with suggestions for the toughest scenario – when there are just the two of you and the skipper goes over the side.

The first point to make about falling off is – DON'T. If there is any possibility of this disaster, everyone should be in lifejackets and harnesses and clipped on. The RNLI advice is to wear lifejackets at all times. They also caution that this is a Mayday scenario. Send a Mayday immediately; don't wait while you spend half an hour trying to recover the casualty. If you do recover him, you can always cancel the Mayday.

MOB procedure for a fully crewed yacht

Five things should happen simultaneously:
1. Shout 'Man Overboard'.
2. Tack, without touching the genoa sheet. This stops the boat dead, in the hove-to position.
3. One person is delegated to point at the MOB throughout the rescue, so you don't lose him.
4. Send a Mayday.
5. Press the MOB Button on the chartplotter or VHF. The machine will give a bearing and distance back to this position (but be aware that the MOB may drift down tide, away from the designated spot).
6. Throw the MOB a lifebuoy or use the throwing line or, in extremis, chuck anything that will help him float.
7. Furl the genoa.
8. Check that there are no ropes overboard.

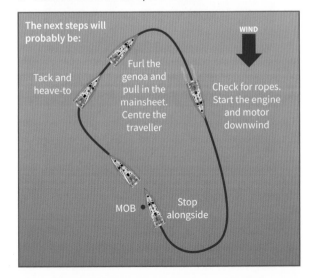

The next steps will probably be:

WIND

Tack and heave-to

Furl the genoa and pull in the mainsheet. Centre the traveller

Check for ropes. Start the engine and motor downwind

MOB •

Stop alongside

9. Start the engine.
10. Consider lowering the mainsail.
11. Motor back to the MOB, just off the wind and pick up on the
    leeward side.

Finally, you will have to retrieve the MOB. There are several
methods:

a. Rig a recovery line from a forward cleat to a sheet winch. The
   casualty steps on it, then is raised slowly as you winch. Don't
   trap their fingers or toes!
b. With the boat alongside the MOB, cut the lines tensioning the
   guardrail and try to drag him aboard.
c. Give him a line and gently pull him to the stern, where he may
   be able to climb aboard using the bathing ladder. Make sure the
   propeller is stationary.
d. Launch the dinghy and pull him aboard that. The liferaft can be
   used in an emergency.
e. Rig up a block and tackle and winch him up, or lead
   a halyard to the windlass.

Whichever is the preferred method on your boat, the key thing is
to have practised it.

Shorthanded procedure: Lifesling method
If you are short-handed this apprach can work well.

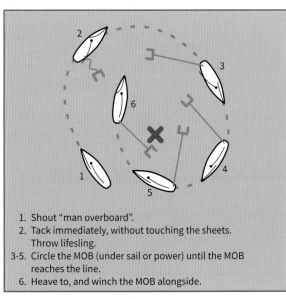

1. Shout "man overboard".
2. Tack immediately, without touching the sheets.
   Throw lifesling.
3-5. Circle the MOB (under sail or power) until the MOB
   reaches the line.
6. Heave to, and winch the MOB alongside.

If the skipper has fallen off while you were asleep, send a Mayday
immediately. Turn the boat through 180 degrees and retrace your
steps on a reciprocal course.

If the skipper is unconscious, don't get into the water yourself. Do
what you can from the yacht, and wait for help.

JARGON BUSTER

Autohelm	A device for steering automatically
Anchor	A device which digs into the seabed and moors the yacht on the end of a chain or line
Backstay	An adjustable wire that pulls the mast aft (and bends it)
Bearing	Orientation in degrees from north
Beating	Zig-zagging towards the wind
Bollard	A short post a boat can be attached to
Boom	Metal tube or wooden spar lying along the bottom of the mainsail
Bow	The forward part of the yacht
Burgee	Flag flown from the masthead
Call sign	Unique identifier used on the VHF radio, e.g. C2JJ8
Capsize	When a boat is turned on its side or over
Chartplotter	Magic box (like a satnav) showing the boat's position and course on a digital chart
Cleat	A projecting fitting for attaching a rope which can be undone easily
Clew	The lower, aft corner of a sail
Close-hauled	Point of sailing closest to the wind
Coachroof	The roof of the saloon
Cockpit	Area where the helm and crew sail the boat
Companionway	The opening leading to the saloon
Dan buoy	A small floating buoy with a flag thrown overboard to mark the position of a Man Overboard
Deck	Top surface of the hull
Docking	Coming into dock / marina
Double	Loop a rope from yacht, around mooring cleat and back to yacht
Downhaul	A rope pulling downwards. The pole downhaul pulls the spinnaker pole downwards
DSC	Digital Selective Calling: the controller, which is a bit like a pager, sends a pulse with your details
Fairlead	Fixed lead to guide a rope or sheet
Foot	The bottom edge of a sail

Foredeck	Part of the deck in front of the mast
Forestay	A fixed wire that pulls the mast forward
Furl	Roll up the sail on the forestay or in the mast or boom
Furling line	Line which furls the sail
Galley	The boat's kitchen
Gennaker	A downwind sail which is a cross between a large genoa and a spinnaker
Genoa	A headsail that overlaps the mast
Goosewinged	Running downwind with the genoa on the opposite side to the mainsail
GPS	The Global Positioning System, based on satellites' signals, gives your latitude and longitude anywhere in the world
Grabrail	A rail on deck or down below to grab hold of
Guardrails	Horizontal wires around the edge of the deck to keep the crew on board
Guy	Windward spinnaker control line
Gybe	A turn where the stern of the boat crosses the wind
Halyard	A rope or wire that hoists a sail
Harness	Item worn (usually as part of the lifejacket). Attach the tether to it when clipping on
Head	The top corner of a sail
Heads	The toilet or toilet compartment
Headsail	Jib or genoa
Head-to-wind	The boat aligned with the bows pointing into the wind and the sails flapping
Helm	Device for steering the boat. Also the person steering
Hove-to	Stopped, with the genoa aback and balancing the mainsail
Jackstay	Wires or lengths of webbing along each side deck. The crew clip on to these to move about the deck safely
Jammer	Deck hardware used to hold a rope under load
Jibsheet	Rope to trim the jib
Keel	Projection under the hull to help stabilise the boat
Kicking strap	Pulley system to pull down on the boom, also called the vang

Latitude	A measurement (in degrees) north or south of the equator. Shown on the vertical scale at the edge of a chart
Leech	The aft (vertical) edge of a sail
Leecloth	A canvas sheet hung to make a 'wall' to keep a sleeper in his bunk
Leeward	The side away from the wind
Lifejacket	Item worn to provide buoyancy when in the water
Lifelines	Webbing straps on the deck to tether onto
Liferaft	An inflatable boat with a canopy, launched when a yacht is in danger of sinking
Longitude	A measurement (in degrees) east or west of the Greenwich meridian. Shown on the horizontal scale at the edge of a chart
Lubber line	The vertical line in front of the compass against which the yacht's heading is read
Luff	The leading edge of a sail
Luff	To turn towards the wind
Mainsail	The sail set on the mast and boom, behind the genoa
Mainsheet	The rope that controls how far the boom, and therefore mainsail, is pulled in
Mayday	Raising the alarm when there is grave and imminent danger to a vessel or person
MOB	Man Overboard
NAVTEX	Electronic device for providing navigational and meteorological information
No go area	An arc 45 degrees either side of the wind diection in which a yacht cannot sail because the sails just flap
Outhaul	A rope or wire that pulls the foot of the mainsail towards the aft end of the boom
Pontoon	Floating dock
Port	Left
Preventer	A rope system for holding the boom out when the yacht is running (preventing a gybe when the yacht rolls)
Pulpit	The stainless steel structure at the bow
Pushpit	The stainless steel structure at the stern
Reaching	Sailing at right angles to the wind

Reefing	Reducing sail area
Roller-reefing	Equipment that allows a sail to be furled
Runners	Adjustable lines from the mast to the corners of the stern. When the windward one is tensioned it pulls the mast back, straightens the mast and straightens the luff of the genoa.
Running	Sailing away from the wind
Rudder	Foil at or near the stern which allows steerage
Sail-tie	A piece of webbing tied around a sail after it has been lowered
Saloon	The living area of a yacht
Seacock	A valve in a pipe, which goes through the hull
Shackle	A metal hoop and pin used to attach one object to another
Sheet	Rope used to trim sails
Shroud	A wire that supports the mast sideways
Skipper	Person in charge of the boat
Slipline	Double line which can be released from onboard and pulled in
Spinnaker	A large downwind sail
Spinnaker pole	Spar to set the spinnaker
Spreader	Horizontal arm projecting from the mast to give a shroud more leverage
Spring	A mooring rope that stops the boat moving forwards or backwards
Squelch	Knob to control level of interference on a VHF radio
Stanchion	A vertical rod that supports the guardrails
Starboard	Right
Stern	The aft part of the boat
Surge	To take the strain off a rope by easing it slightly
Tack	A turn where the bow of the boat turns through the wind
Tack	The lower, forward corner of a sail
Tack line	Rope attached to the tack of a sail
Tailing	Keeping tension on a rope which has gone around a winch
Take a turn	Loop a rope once around
Telltale	A streamer on a sail to show the flow of air
Tethered	Tied

Toerail	Lip round the edge of the deck
Topping lift	A rope running from the end of the boom via the top of the mast and down to a cleat, used to lift the boom
Traveller	A slider on a track to which the mainsheet attaches, used to move the boom to windward or leeward
Trimming	Adjusting the sails to suit the wind
Uphaul	A rope pulling upwards. The pole uphaul pulls up the spinnaker pole
Vang	A pulley system to pull down on the boom. Also called the kicking strap
VHF	Radio for communication (very high frequency)
Watch	Period of time allocated to part of the crew to be responsible for the boat and its progress
Waypoint	A position defined by longitude and latitude which can be displayed as a cross on an electronic chart, marking the boat's final or intermediate destination
Winch	A mechanical device to help wind in a rope, using a winch handle
Windex	A pivoted arrow at the top of the mast indicating the wind direction
Windlass	A machine for winding up the anchor chain
Windward	The side towards the wind